SAM, SARA, ETC.

A play in two acts

by

Brian Arundel

Červená Barva Press
Somerville, Massachusetts

Copyright © 2021 by Brian Arundel

All rights reserved. No part of this book may be reproduced in any manner without written consent except for the quotation of short passages used inside of an article, criticism, or review.

Červená Barva Press
P.O. Box 440357
W. Somerville, MA 02144-3222

www.cervenabarvapress.com

Bookstore: www.thelostbookshelf.com

Cover art and design: William J. Kelle

ISBN: 978-1-950063-43-7

Library of Congress Control Number: 2021933045

samsara (səmˈsɑːrə) *n. Hinduism & Buddhism* **1.** The eternal cycle of birth, suffering, death, and rebirth. **2.** The transmigration or rebirth of a person.

In memory of Jerry Eugene McGlown

Sam, Sara, Etc. was first performed on September 13, 2010, by Orfeo Theatre Company in Boston, with the following cast.

Sam………………………………… Risher Reddick

Sara………………………………… Georgia Lyman*

Rita………………………………...Cheryl McMahon*

Ward……………………………….Will Lyman

Chloe……………………………….Liz Hayes*

Cody………………………………..Daniel Berger-Jones

Meredith……………………………Anna Waldron

*Actors appeared courtesy of Actors' Equity Association

CHARACTERS

SAM	In his early 30s.
SARA Late 20s.	Sam's cynical sister, a recovering addict.
RITA	Their mother, trying to remain upbeat. Pushing 60.
WARD	The father, a fisherman, proud but getting desperate. A few years older than Rita.
CHLOE	The driven host of a television show, in her 30s.
CODY	Chloe's cameraman, in his late 20s.
MEREDITH	Sam's estranged wife. Early 30s.

TIME

The present. Late autumn.

PLACE

A country house near water.

SETTING

The house has seen better days; it was decorated more than thirty years ago and hasn't changed since. Front door upstage left, living room at left, kitchen upstage right with a small dining table center right. Windows on each side wall. Stairs climb upstage wall to a landing, with a hallway opening beneath. Stacks of newspapers are scattered randomly throughout living room. Three-by-five cards are taped to various objects. An open backpack in the corner.

ACT I

Scene 1

(AT RISE: Stage is dark save for a spotlight on SAM, wearing a homemade superhero outfit with a large "T" on the chest and headphones over his ears. He is obviously frightened. He stands on a chair holding a coil of rope in his hand, frantically trying to toss it over a beam above. From offstage we hear an unidentifiable, menacing sound of something large and heavy, perhaps a massive limping beast alternately sliding and stomping closer, accompanied by the sound of SAM's amplified, racing heartbeat and murmuring voices.

SAM succeeds in getting the rope over the beam and slips the noose around his neck. The menacing sound is closer. SAM prepares himself. Just as he is about to jump off the chair, a phone rings. It takes a few beats for him to notice as sounds—the phone ringing, his heartbeat, voices, the sliding and stomping—crescendo.

Finally, SAM pulls a cell phone from somewhere in his outfit. As soon as he opens it, the sounds stop. He removes the headphones from his hears (after initially forgetting about them) and answers the cell.

SAM

Hello? This is he. (*beat*) How did you get this number? I did? I see. You know, I'm a little occupied at the moment. (*beat*) No, sorry, I don't believe I'll be renewing my subscription. (beat) No, really... Because—yes, I understand. But really it's—yes, that's true. (casually) Well, that is a very good offer. OK, fine. Put me down for one more year. The same card. Yes. Thank you.

(Hangs up. The sounds suddenly begin again, louder. He putshis headphones back on and again prepares to jump. Phone rings again.)

Oh come on!

(He removes his headphones and answers the cell. Again, the noises stop.)
Hello? No, I'm sorry. Meredith is no longer available at this number. And I don't know where she is. (beat) I'm alone. Goodbye.

(SAM hangs up, turns off and pockets phone. For a few beats, total silence. Then only a loud, deliberate and heavy banging on the door. SAM, terrified, prepares to jump. He looks up, grabs rope, tugs a little to test it, then tugs harder. The rope, not properly tied above, cascades down around him. Everything goes silent. He stands for a moment, looking hopeless.)

BLACKOUT

Scene 2

(RITA pours water into tea kettle and places it on stove to heat. She looks at refrigerator, pauses, then opens a drawer and pulls out a magic marker and small piece of sticky. She writes on the paper and sticks it to the refrigerator. Satisfied, she turns and looks out the window.
SARA enters while knocking.)

SARA
Is he awake yet?

RITA
Not yet. Still sleeps like the dead.

SARA
How's he doing?

RITA
About as well as you'd expect. Never could understand why he married that woman. I suppose it's true that love is blind.

SARA
I'll never forget their wedding. Not every day you see a couple's first dance performed as an interpretive bridal solo.

RITA
Yes, that was a little bizarre.

SARA
And the way she always flirted with any male not in a wheelchair.

RITA
Well, no matter what, we shouldn't ask him about whatever happened. He can tell us in his own time, when he's ready. We must be tactful. He's been through a lot.

(SAM enters in a bathrobe. As he passes refrigerator he notices the piece of paper, appears momentarily confused, and moves on.)

RITA
Good morning, dear. How're you feeling?

SAM
Like I've been eaten and regurgitated. (beat) I'd forgotten how the sounds are here. It's very comforting. Same bird songs. The wind in the leaves sounds just like I remember. Even the Flaherty's dog.

SARA
Actually that's a different dog. The old Brutus got hit by the ice cream truck but the Flaherty's just bought a dog that looked exactly the same.

RITA
That's a different dog?

SAM
Is there anything to eat? I'm starving.

RITA
I have a pie in the oven. Pecan. Your favorite.

SARA
You got up this morning to make pie?

RITA
Oh no, course not. It was frozen.

(RITA gets SAM a piece of pie.)

SARA
So what happened with Meredith?

(RITA gives her sharp look, to which SARA shrugs defensively.)

SAM
Meredith and I are no longer . . .

(Both RITA and SARA are initially pleased before lapsing into compassion for SAM.)

SARA (pleasantly)
No longer . . . ?

SAM
I'll let her explain.
(SAM removes note from pocket and reads it.)
"Dear Sam." This is where it gets a little ambiguous.

SAM
"I'm sorry, but I can't be with you anymore. I don't wantto cause you pain, but I'm leaving, and chances are you'll never see me again."
That could be her just being dramatic.
"I feel that I've lost my identity; I don't know who I am anymore. I must leave and follow wherever the universe will take me. I need to explore the landscapes of my mind to find my true self."
She's obviously just going through some sort of stage, don't you think? (beat) What do you think it means, 'landscapes of my mind'?

SARA (skeptically)
"The universe" is going to take care of her?

RITA
You poor thing. When did this happen?

SAM
Twenty-seven days ago.

RITA
That's almost a month.

SARA
Well done, Mother.

RITA
You didn't say anything for a whole month?

SAM
I sort of lost track of time.

SARA
Well, I for one say good riddance.

RITA
Sara, that's not very sisterly. (beat) Though I have to admit you might have a point.

SAM
Really.

RITA
While you may have loved her, sadly, Meredith is a very unbalanced woman who obviously needs help. And most importantly, from now on that little hippie will be inflicting her twisted psychosis on someone other than my son for a change.

SARA
Exceptionally tactful, Mother.

RITA
Just my opinion. Actresses . . . they spend all their time pretending to be someone else. No wonder they're all a little loose in the head. And in other ways.

SAM
Meredith doesn't act anymore. She said she could no longer embrace a "disarticulated self." She teaches yoga now.

RITA
Acting, yoga . . . What does that woman have against a legitimate profession? (beat) Sam, I think you just need to get out and socialize. You know, I saw Paula Sullivan the other day at the grocery store. She said her daughter Sally's moved back to town.

SAM
Sally Sullivan? Mother we went to a dance once in seventh grade. What am I going to say to her, "Good to see you, Sally, it's been awhile. Say, I see you've grown some breasts since then"?
(Pause. SAM moves to kitchen window and looks out.)
A month ago I had all the things you're supposed to have: I owned my own business, I had a wife everybody liked, a little two-bedroom house with a wraparound porch. Meredith and I would sit on the back porch sipping wine and looking at birch trees, talking about what things might be like when we got old. (beat) Now I'm afraid to be alone in the house. And when the sun sets, the birch trees look like a wall of black eyes. (beat) Mother, I appreciate your effort, but I'm not going to ask out Sally Sullivan.

(RITA sets cups on table. Each has a piece of paper sticking to it. SAM is perplexed, SARA has no reaction.)

SAM
This is the mug I had as a kid.

RITA
I've kept all your things. Mugs, plates, little spoons from when you were babies. Your clothes. Teeth that fell out.

SARA
You kept our teeth?

RITA
Of course.

SARA
Isn't that a little macabre?

RITA
It's tradition. Like bronzed booties.

SARA
Oh god I hated those things.

SAM
Your booties?

SARA
When I was a little I thought they were some poor kid's real feet. I always wondered what you and Dad had done with the rest of the body.

(RITA pours tea. SAM picks up card taped to chair.)

SAM
"Se-die-a."

RITA
That's "SAY-dee-a." It means "chair."

                          SARA
Mom's taking Italian.

   (RITA writes on a piece of paper and sticks it on SAM's bathrobe.)

                          RITA
Figlio.

                          SAM
Is Dad taking it with you?

                          RITA
That'll be the day.

                          SARA
Well who knows, maybe one day you'll meet a strapping Italian man who can't speak English and needs help with directions.

                     RITA (mischievously)
And he'll be hungry.

(Rita catches herself as the door opens and WARD enters with the mail and an armload of newspapers. He sets them down and holds on to the mail, opening an envelope.)

                          RITA
That took longer than expected.

                          WARD
Was working on the boat. Needs a new coat of bottom primer and the NAV system is acting up again.

   (He reads one of the pieces of mail, mutters to himself angrily and shakes head, then stuffs the paper in his coat.)

SARA

You were out in this weather?

WARD

Weather makes no difference to a fisherman.

SAM

How's it been? The fishing.

WARD

Little slow. Truck's stuttering again too, even though that mechanic had it forever. You know, I bet mechanics don't even own cars themselves. They just take turns driving ours around all week.
   (to RITA)
Hear anything?

RITA

Not yet.

WARD

   (to himself)
Supposed to call any day now.

SAM

Hear what?

SARA

   (to SAM)
Oh, you'll love this.

RITA

Ward's entering us in some sweepstakes. For television.

SAM

Sweepstakes?

(WARD picks up random newspaper and opens it up to display cutout portion of a page, which he looks through.)

WARD
And I cornered the market on the entries. For the past couple of weeks I've been all over town collecting newspapers. That's the thing, see—limit the competition. Foolproof.

(RITA writes a note and attaches it to the stack of newspapers.)

RITA
Giornali.

SAM
(to SARA)
What's he talking about?

SARA
The local station is running a contest for working families. The winners will star in some kind of weekly reality show.

WARD
It's not a reality show. It's a documentary. It's serious.

SARA
Whatever. The show's supposed to air all summer for the six or seven folks who still watch network television.

SAM
Mom, you went along with this?

(RITA shrugs.)

WARD
Of course she did. Your mother would love to be on television. And the best part: contestants receive ten thousand dollars. Cash.

RITA
Winners receive the money, dear. Not just the contestants.

WARD (dismissively)
You don't know all the details.

(SAM, incredulous, looks at SARA.)

SARA
Don't look at me. I don't live here.

SAM
You only live a block away. They can still find you.

SARA
A block and a half. With tall hedges in between. (beat) Luckily the odds are about a zillion to one.

SAM
Sounds just a little crazy to me.

WARD
(approaching SAM threateningly)
Crazy? Who you calling crazy?

SAM
I just said—

WARD (angrily)
I'm trying to do something for this family. And just maybe this could get a little recognition for fishermen to boot. Men out there on boats working hard, fishing in any kind of

weather trying to feed this country. But you wouldn't know anything about that, would you?

RITA

Ward.

WARD

No you wouldn't. You sit all day in your little shop selling coffee to bums and hobnobbing with hippies.

SARA

Do people still hobnob?

SAM

It's a living.

WARD

It's a dead end. Fishing puts food on tables. It's honest work. And we're the ones getting regulated out of business on account of those damn lying lobby groups.
    (Pause. Unsure where to direct his frustration)
And you showing up in the middle of the night without so much as a phone call.

RITA

Ward!

    (Pause.)

WARD (relenting)

Point is we can win this thing. Why not us? We stand as good a chance as anyone. Better. That's what's great about this country: opportunity. Anyone can win. It's the American Dream.

SARA
I thought the American Dream was more about hard work than pure luck.

WARD
(to SAM)
We're going to have to figure out what to do with you though.

SAM
What do you mean?

WARD
Didn't expect you to just show up out of nowhere. You're not listed in the application form so you're not in the cast. We'll have to explain who you are.

SAM
Well, how about I just be who I am?

WARD
That ain't gonna work.

RITA
We can deal with that later, Ward. If we're selected.

WARD
Oh, we'll win all right. We're going to win. That's a fact.

RITA
Well. Until then let's just avoid the excitement. I think Sam could use some peace and quiet.

(WARD hesitates uncomfortably before SAM.)

WARD
Yes. Well. (beat). I told you that woman was no good.

RITA		SARA
Ward!	Dad.	

                    SAM

No you didn't.

                    WARD

Sure I did. Just before you had that confusing wedding.

                    SAM

No. You didn't.

   (Pause.)

                    WARD

You just don't remember.

                    SAM

You never said anything like that.

                    WARD

Yes I did, goddammit, you just didn't hear me! (beat) Still. S'pose you might as well just go ahead and stay here as long as you need to.

                    RITA

Of course he can. I've already told him that.

                    WARD (awkwardly)

Well. It's not a problem at all, that's all I'm saying. You just gotta tough it out.

                    SARA

"Tough it out?" He didn't sprain his ankle, Dad.

WARD
I understand that. I'm not deaf. I'm just saying . . . A man rides the rough waves. Stands tall on deck and rides out the storm. Gotta turn the boat into the winds.

   (Pause.)

SAM
Thanks. I'll keep all that in mind.

SARA
Yes, clichés are comforting at times like this.

WARD (obliviously)
But things are about to get better, that's a fact. The silver lining is right around the corner. (beat) I'm going to go wash up. I'd like to have some of that bacon you're making.

RITA
It's pie, Ward.

WARD
Pie? Smells like bacon.

   (WARD exits upstairs.)

SARA
I swear that man's light bulb is getting dimmer every day.

SAM
Mom, this is one of the most ridiculous schemes I've ever heard. A contest for a reality show? The only saving grace is the odds against you actually winning it.

RITA
Ward seemed to think it was a good idea. (beat) At least he's trying.

SARA
What, to get committed? Come on Mother, he's buying up newspapers all over town?

RITA
Perhaps this is a path God wants us to follow. Who am I to question?

SARA
A person with a brain, that's who.

RITA
Though the truth is, times are a little tough.

SAM
How tough?

RITA
Tough enough. But it's just a test. God doesn't give us anything we can't handle.

SARA
So where does that leave the Agnostics?

RITA
Sara, please.

SAM
Has the fishing been bad?

RITA
Who knows.

SAM
What's that supposed to mean?

                    RITA
He hasn't fished with that boat in two years.

                    SARA
You're kidding.

                    RITA
He's sold off his quota each season. Prices they're getting barely cover the cost of fuel.

                    SAM
So he's getting paid not to fish.

                    RITA
Basically. Those big factory ships can afford to buy up all the quotas. They're just going to drive everyone out of business.

                    SAM
Wouldn't it be better to just sell the boat?

                    RITA
Ward will never sell that boat. You know how he is. It's who he is. (beat) We were going to go to Alaska, years ago. Crabbers were making money hand over fist. Ward was going to fish a few years, and we were going to take that money and retire early. Travel places. Ward said he'd take me to Rome.

                    SARA
And?

                    RITA
And just like that it was over. The crabs were gone before we could even get there, and suddenly we had two kids and a mortgage.
    (Pause. SAM watches here intently.)
Listen to me. I don't know how I got off on this.

SAM
Mom, let me ask you something: when it's quiet, what do you hear?

RITA
What's that?

SAM
What do you hear when it's quiet?

RITA
I don't think I understand, Sam.

SAM
Never mind, I was just thinking out loud.

RITA
Quiet is quiet, isn't it?

SAM
Of course.

(RITA hugs SAM hard.)

RITA
Poor Sam. (beat) You just tell me what you'd like to eat for dinner. I'll go shopping as soon as I go change.

(RITA rises, stops, writes on a piece of paper and sticks it to the wall, then exits upstairs.)

SARA (dryly)
(to SAM)
Welcome home.

BLACKOUT

Scene 3

(Fifteen minutes later. SARA and SAM are sitting at the kitchen table. She is eating pie; a piece sits untouched before SAM, who looks dejected.)

SARA
Yessirree, nobody can heat up a frozen pie quite like Mom.

SAM
Remember shucking all that corn? We used to sit here for hours. You and me, right here at the table. Shucking ear after ear into a brown paper bag.

SARA
I remember how those little strings between the kernels made me think of pubic hairs.

SAM
Think I just changed my mind about getting some corn.

(Pause. SARA thinks for a beat, then holds out her hand, palm up, as if waiting for something. SAM doesn't understand.)

SARA
Your wedding day? At the reception. (beat) When we were dancing?
(Pause. SAM still isn't making the connection.)
You owe me a dollar.

(SAM thinks, remembers, and bitterly reaches into his pocket.)

SAM
All I have is change.

(SAM tosses change in her direction, onto the table.)

SARA

That's fine. I hear change is good.

SAM

When did you become so cynical?

SARA

I consider myself a realist.

SAM

So you bet my marriage would fail.

SARA

I figured it was even money so I took a shot. (beat) I meant it as a joke.

SAM

I'm dying laughing. Turns out my marriage was the joke. (beat) Maybe you just don't want to see anyone happy. Maybe you want everyone to be as miserable as you are.

SARA

That's some deep analysis there, Doc. But I don't have to want people to be miserable. Look around, Sam. Everybody suffers. It's life.
   (Pause.)
I'm sorry she left you. Really.

SAM

I can hear everything in the house now.

SARA

I imagine it's pretty quiet.

SAM

But it's not, not really. That's just it: It's like the house has come alive.

SARA

No, dear brother, you're just hearing things because it's quieter.

SAM

This is different. This isn't your everyday wood settling or furnace knocking. I can hear the walls breathing. I can hear the house's heartbeat. It's frightening.

SARA

Oh, I see. I didn't realize you were legitimately losing your mind.

SAM

I don't know what I'm losing.

SARA

Look, Sam, not to be insensitive, but a lot of marriages fail. Hell, Mom and Dad's should've failed a long time ago. As impossible as it sounds, you will get through this.

SAM

It's not like a thunderstorm. It's not like I ride it out until the sun returns. She's not coming back, I realize that. I've just got to get used to the dark I guess. And the noise. Just don't know if I can. (beat) Did you know that turtles don't hear sound the same way we do?

SARA

Turtles?

SAM

They have the inner ear mechanisms, they just don't have the outer ear to amplify anything. They sense vibrations. Have a great sense of smell. But they don't hear as well as we do.

SARA

Is that a fact.

SAM

It is. I've developed a fondness for turtles over the years. Fascinating creatures.

SARA

Cheaper than a dog I guess. Though maybe not so good with a frisbee.

(SAM goes to refrigerator and reads a note before opening it.)

SAM

Got to be something else in the "il frigorifero."
(He takes a bag of grapes out of the fridge.)
These look completely rotten.

SARA

Not surprised. Mom tends to keep fruit around 'til it's covered in fur.

(SAM places a bag or trash can at a distance. While speaking they will take turns throwing grapes into it, perhaps gradually increasing the difficulty of shots. The feeling is familiar, as if these two often played such games when they were younger.)

SARA

So . . .

                    SAM
Look, I know I'm not going to die from grief. I'm not going to kill myself or anything. Don't think I could do it right anyway.

                    SARA (surprised)
OK...

                    SAM
There are other fish in the... whatever. It's just... one day your life's headed in one direction, it's all under control, you know what to expect. And then the next... It's all just less real somehow... Like I'm only seeing pictures of my life, and I'm not really in it at all.

                    SARA
Sam, you're still you. You can't just always define your life in terms of someone else. Or something else.

                    SAM
Where'd you get that piece of advice?

                    SARA
Talk radio, where else? But it makes sense. Like, when someone asks who you are, what do you say?

                    SAM
What do you... my name.

                    SARA
I mean besides that.

                    SAM
Sam... well, used to be Meredith's husband.

                    SARA
See, that's what I mean.

SAM
I own a coffee shop.
   (SARA makes 'keep going' gestures)
My age. Where I went to school . . .

SARA
Right. They're all symptoms.

(Pause.)

SAM
So what about you, then?

SARA
Haven't the faintest clue. But at least I'm aware of it.
   (SAM looks at her incredulously.)
What? It's a start.

(Pause.)

SAM
I found out Meredith was having an affair.

SARA
Well, there's a surprise. (beat) Sorry.

SAM
Actually more than one, if I'm not mistaken.

SARA
What makes you think that?

SAM
Few things here and there. Suspicious emails. Hushed phone conversations. Catching her a few times at parties making out

with various individuals. (beat) The clincher may've been finding a condom underneath the couch.

SARA

And I take it—

SAM

Neon green isn't my color. And yes—it was used. She'd finally found her Prince Charming.

SARA

Doesn't sound so charming to me.

SAM

No, that was his actual name online. His avatar looked like one of the Three Musketeers. He rode around on a white horse and spoke in courtly English.

SARA

So Meredith was a nerd, too.

SAM

She dabbled. (beat) My therapist has suggested I take up meditation. He says it'll help calm my mind, get perspective.

SARA

Has it?

SAM

Hell no, it drives me insane. When you stop to listen, there's nothing but noise. Like a beehive. I feel much saner when I'm drastically out of touch with myself. (beat) He told me in some Japanese temples, monks walk around and beat people with sticks to keep them focused.

SARA
Can't imagine that going over too well here. We sue when our coffee's too hot. (beat) Could always ask Dad to help with that, I'm sure he'd be happy to oblige. (beat; SARA is immediately regretful) Sorry.

SAM (shrugging)
Maybe some folks do need to have some self-awareness beaten into them. Our delusion beaten out of them, I don't know which.

(Pause.)

SARA
I imagine Mom would say something about it all being part of God's plan. You know, like tsunamis and wars and all those godlike things.

SAM
I thought recovering addicts were supposed to be big on faith.

SARA
Many do join the God squad, it's true.

SAM
But never you?

SARA
At first being sober is like learning to walk, so it helps if you have a crutch. But some of us just have a harder time with that particular delusion. (beat) God isn't going to stop me from drinking; I do that.

SAM
I take it at Christmas you'll be sticking with "Seasons Greetings" cards.

SARA
I'm actually thinking of switching to "Happy Boxing Day."

(The bag of grapes is empty.)

SAM
We seem to be out of grapes. But once again I believe I was victorious.

SARA
Not a chance. You just don't have any balls.
(SARA produces one more grape and tosses it toward target.)
Poor Sam. Lost again.

BLACKOUT

Scene 4

(Later that evening. Dinner WARD, RITA, SAM and SARA play charades in the living room. WARD is drinking. SAM is in the middle of his turn and prances about flamboyantly.)

SARA

"Lord of the Dance"!

(She is partly correct. SAM motions to her to "shorten" the title.)

RITA

Oh, that Mr. Flatley. Mama mia.

WARD

He's a nancy.

(SAM puts hands together overhead to form a big 'O'.)

RITA

Oh, the Olympics!

SARA

Rings! "Lord of the Rings!"
(SARA is correct. SAM and RITA applaud. It's SARA's turn. She mimes "film," "two words," "first word." She joins her hands behind her back and holds her elbows out.)

WARD

(getting drunk)
Looks like Mrs. Butterworth.

(SARA, frustrated, flaps her elbows.)

SAM

"March of the Penguins"!

RITA

"The Flying Nun"?

(SARA mimes a "halo" over her head.)

SAM

"Angel . . . "?

SARA, SAM, RITA

"Moby Dick."

SARA
(immediately preparing to leave)
Well, that's it for me.

WARD

I didn't even do anything.

SARA

Dad, you always do the same thing. It's either "Moby Dick" or "The Old Man and the Sea."

WARD

No I don't.

SAM

Well, there was a Christmas a few years back when he did "A Perfect Storm."

RITA

There was that one time he did "Shoes of the Fisherman."

SARA
Until he found out the movie had nothing to do with fishing.

WARD
Well so what if I do? Nothing wrong with that. Jesus was a fisherman. And his disciples. Fishing was our first industry.

SAM
I thought that was bartending.

SARA
I think prostitution.

WARD
No goddammit! Fishing! Before we grew anything, we caught fish. Fishermen feed the nation. It's the noblest profession.

SAM
But you don't even fish.

(Pause. RITA looks shocked.)

WARD (menacingly)
What did you say?

SAM
I said you don't even fish. Mom told us you've been selling your allocations.

(Pause. WARD looks fiercely at RITA before turning to SAM.)

WARD
I've sold a few allocations. For now. Because there's no money out there right now. It ain't worth it. They're paying pennies for the pound. And we got bills to pay.

SARA
From what I hear there's no fish out there to catch.

WARD
Oh there's fish out there. Plenty. But the damn government officials and scientists want everyone to believe there's nothing out there, put us all out of business. Then next thing you know, the corporations'll come in with the big factory trawlers and scoop up the whole damn ocean floor. (beat) There's fish out there. I know there is.
   (to SAM)
And don't you be telling me about fishing. Cried like a goddamn baby last time you were on a boat.
   (to RITA)
Remember the first time I took him fishing?

RITA
Ward.

WARD
Stood right next to the damn trawl door and got his foot caught in the line. Nearly went overboard. Now you're afraid of water for chrissake.

RITA
Ward, he nearly drowned.

WARD
And I lost a whole trawl net full of fish! (beat) My own offspring, afraid of water.

SAM (meekly)
I never said I was a fisherman.

WARD
Goddamn right you're not a fisherman. Worst excuse for one I've ever seen. Got no business on a deck. Hell, you'd he'd be

better off as bait. (beat) And no fisherman. Ain't even much of a man.

                    RITA (warning)
Ward.

                    WARD
Well it's true ain't it?

                    SAM
Who cares?

                    WARD
    (turning toward SAM)
What did you say?

                    SAM
I said who cares about fishing? It's a dead end.

    (WARD grabs SAM and prepares to hit him.)

                    RITA
Ward!

    (All are frozen for a moment. Phone rings. WARD stands for a few beats, staring at SAM, before going to the kitchen to answer it. His conversation is inaudible, but he writes on a pad of paper.)

                    SARA
    (to RITA)
When did Dad become an asshole?

                    RITA
    (absently admonishing)
Sara. Your father's been under a lot of pressure.

(WARD hangs up and comes back to living room, triumphant, waving a piece of paper.)

WARD

Who's crazy now?!

BLACKOUT

Scene 5

(The following evening. SAM, RITA, WARD, SARA, CODY and CHLOE sit in living room. CODY is around SARA's age and dressed casually; he holds a folder of papers. CHLOE is vain, dressed elegantly and speaks with a certain theatrical arrogance.

SAM, WARD, SARA and RITA all have stickers on their shirts.)

CHLOE
What we're going for here is reality.

CODY
Definitely, reality.

CHLOE
(waving hand generally around room)
So we might have to make a few changes

RITA
What sort of changes.

(RITA rises and sticks a piece of paper on CHLOE.)

CHLOE
(confused by paper)
Just cosmetic. Different colors. Maybe a dog.

WARD
A dog?

CODY
Or two.

RITA
Absolutely not. We can't have a dog.

(RITA sticks paper to CODY.)

CHLOE

I know you're not experienced with such things, but I am. And I know one thing for sure: Sometimes sacrifices have to be made if you want to have a chance to be a star.

SAM

Explain this to me again.

CHLOE

And you are?

SAM

Sam.
    (beat; points to name tag, then speaks with "rabbit ears")
I'm "the son."

(CHLOE looks to CODY, who rifles through papers on a clipboard, then shakes his head.)

CHLOE

I'm sorry but we don't see you.

SAM

I'm right here.

CODY

You're not in our file.

CHLOE

Which means you don't exist.

SAM

Don't exist?

WARD
We weren't expecting him. Can't we just say he's a neighbor?

RITA
Cousin? From Idaho. Sells insurance.

CODY
I'll see what I can do about getting . . . ?

SAM
Sam.

CHLOE
"Sam." I don't know. We might have to change that.

SAM
Change my name?

CHLOE
(to CODY)
Gimme a name.

CODY
(reading quickly from list)
Hank, Dirk, Daryll, Rutger, Hans, Cyril, Sheldon, Phinneas, Omar—

SARA (sarcastically)
Oh, definitely Phinneas.

CHLOE
He does look a bit like a Cyril. Well, we'll figure it out. Main thing is you need to fill out your bios on the sheet that Cody will give you.
(CODY stands and passes out papers)

These will give us a better sense of your characters. Your motivations. Who you are, all that nonsense. (beat) Over the next day or two we'll shoot a few demo scenes, a "get to know you" tape. This will be the main part of your application.

WARD
Wait, you mean this isn't a done deal?

CHLOE
A done—what?

CODY
This is the last stage of selection. You and two other families are finalists.

WARD
So we haven't won?

(Pause. CHLOE looks from WARD to CODY and back.)

CHLOE (to all)
The important thing is you look like you're acting naturally. Don't worry, we'll help you with that. Just remember that whatever it is we tell you to do, make it seem like you do that thing all the time.

RITA
I'm sorry, I'm not sure I follow. Non ho capito.

CHLOE
Right. Go with that.
    (to SARA)
You.

SARA

Sara.

CHLOE

That could work. Now about your clothes.

SARA

What about them?

CHLOE

They look sort of . . .

(CHLOE snaps her fingers at CODY for a word.)

CODY

Casually elegant, stylishly understated, subtly beguiling?

CHLOE

I was thinking more frumpy and homely.

SARA

Excuse me?

CHLOE

You know, a little plain. Dowdy. Light on the makeup and . . . other things.

SARA

Whereas you obviously prefer to emulate circus clowns.

CODY

(to SARA)
I think you look fine. I mean, you're . . . not homely at all.

(SARA gives CODY a look of surprised gratitude.)

CHLOE
Nothing personal. We'll work on that. In any case, we'll shoot the vid, maybe two, clean it up a little and submit it.

SAM
Submit it to whom?

CHLOE
"To whom." That's so cute. We submit it to the producer.

WARD
So when is it on TV?

CODY
The winner gets on television.

WARD
Well, what about the money?

CHLOE
Money.

WARD
Yeah, when do we get it?

CODY
You get the money if you get the show.

WARD
And we don't get the show—

CHLOE
Unless yours is the video chosen, correct.

WARD
I'm not sure that's what the rules said.

(CODY passes out packets.)

                    CHLOE
OK, these are your legal forms—disclaimers, liability waivers, permissions, all that.

                    RITA
What are we signing?

                    CHLOE
Your life away. Kidding. Basically this absolves the network of responsibility for various mishaps, natural disasters, demonic possession, etc., etc., and essentially gives them the rights to you.

                    SAM
What do you mean rights to us?

                    CODY
For ads and whatnot. To use your images. Your identities.

                    RITA
You'd own our identities?

                    CHLOE
Not me, personally. Where would I fit them all? Just a joke. The network owns them.

                    RITA
    (to WARD)
I'm not sure I like that.

                    WARD
I'm sure it's standard procedure.

CHLOE

Course it is.
   (to WARD)
Now you. Ward. You are a fisherman.

WARD (proudly)

That's right. All my life. As was my father and his father.

CHLOE

That's a tough sell.

WARD

   (not hearing her)
I see this as an opportunity to talk about the industry, the struggle of today's fishermen, having to deal with government bureaucrats, environmental lobby groups—

CHLOE

Yes, yes, that's all good.

WARD

There's a lot to cover.

CHLOE

And we'll get to that.
   (to RITA)
Rita. You are a . . . what?

RITA

I'm a housewife.

CHLOE

Really.

RITA

Yes.

CHLOE
That is just adorable. So you, what . . . cook and . . . stuff?

RITA
Yes, I do.

CHLOE
By choice? Or is this between jobs?

RITA
If housework is the vocation that God's chosen for me, I'll do it happily.

SARA
Mom puts the 'fun' in 'fundamentalism.'

CHLOE
Fascinating. I think we can make that work. Throw in some patriotism. Maybe hang a flag.

SARA
Oh, brother.

(CHLOE points to SARA, forgetting her name. SARA holds up name tag.)

CODY
Sara.

CHLOE
Right. What is it you do?

SARA
I help run a shelter for recovering addicts.

CODY
(impressed)

Social work?

CHARACTER: SARA
(interested)
You could call it that.

CHLOE
(trying to intrude)
Though if you think about it, who doesn't do "social" work?

CODY
Mimes?

CHLOE
(not amused; to SARA:)
And what drew you to that . . . profession?

SARA
I'm a recovering addict.

CHLOE
Oh that's excellent!
(to CODY)
Make a big note. "Junkie."

SARA
"Addict." Recovering.

CHLOE
Whatever.
(to CODY)
We've got to really push that.
(to SARA)
Recovery. So I take it you're an evangelical as well?

SARA
Hardly.

WARD

She's a goddamn atheist.

RITA
Ward, please don't swear like that.

CHLOE (fascinated)
Really? An atheist?

SARA

Swear to god.

CHLOE
These addicts of yours. Are they poor?

SARA

Mostly.

CHLOE

Homeless?

SARA

A few.

CHLOE
Fantastic. Maybe you could bring some home.

RITA
She doesn't actually live here. She lives a few blocks away.

SARA
Yeah, and I'm afraid I already sold them all.

CHLOE
You don't think you could, say, take one out for a walk and happen to drop in?

SARA
They're not pets!

CHLOE
Impressive. Impassioned. I like it.

SARA
Bite me.

CHLOE
Excuse me?

SAM
Jesus, Mom.

RITA
A C-section baby. He just curled his little fists and started banging at his cage, just demanding to be released. Couldn't wait to get out and start living.

CHLOE
Is that a fact.

RITA
Sara on the other hand, she didn't want to come out at all. They practically needed the "jaws of life" to pull her out.

CHLOE (sarcastically)
I'm sure we can do something with that. (beat) So, Sam. For work. What do you do?

SAM
I run a business.

CHLOE
OK. What kind of business?

WARD (bitterly)
He runs a damn coffee shop.

CHLOE
A coffee shop. And how does this make you feel? You know, being in the service industry at your age?

SAM
Being in the . . . ? I own the café.

CHLOE (considering)
OK. Blue-collar, small-business owner. Americans love their coffee, etc., etc. I think we can get some identification with that. Sympathy too, given your age. (beat) And you've lived in your parents' house all your life?

SAM
All my . . . what? No. I'm visiting.

CHLOE (skeptically)
Sure. Girlfriends?

SAM (hesitantly)
No.

CHLOE

Not bad, not bad. We can work with that. Oh, that's very good. You are truly in sad shape. In the right light, you could be quite pathetic.

                    WARD
            Ain't that the truth.

                    CHLOE
Americans love pathetic. We'll talk more later. In greater detail. But I think we're onto something here.
    (CHLOE stands while CODY collects papers.)
All right people, I think we have all the preliminary information we need for now.

                    WARD
So what happens next?

                    CHLOE
Well, we get some construction workers to come level the house and build a set in its place, then we'll hire some actors to play all of you. (beat) Kidding! I'm kidding.

                    CODY
We'll be back bright and early with a camera, makeup, some lights and whatnot. Start filming. Easy as pie.

                    CHLOE
You won't even know we're here.

                    CODY
We'll shoot a few takes, collect the samples and see what we have.

                    CHLOE (to SARA)
Don't worry, not those kind of samples. (SARA reacts) Joke!

WARD

All sounds good to me.

(CHLOE and CODY prepare to leave.)

CODY (sincerely, to SARA)

It was nice meeting you.

SARA (surprised)

You too.

RITA

I'll be sure to have some coffee for you when you arrive. And maybe some pie.

CHLOE

That won't be necessary.

RITA

It's not a problem. The pie is frozen and the coffee's instant.

CHLOE

(to CODY)
Come along.

RITA

Arriverderli i miei amici.

(They exit, looking oddly at RITA.)

SARA

Are you sure about this, Dad?

WARD

Never been surer of anything in my life.

                        RITA
Really?

                         SAM
I still think this is completely crazy.

                        WARD
There you go again. Talking about failure. All you ever talk about is failure.

                         SAM
You're putting everyone through this nonsense for *nothing*. This whole plan is insane.

                        WARD
You know what you are?

                         SAM
I can't wait to hear.

                        WARD
You're a *loser*. You can't help it, you're just too afraid to take a chance. *Loser*.

                        RITA
Ward, that's enough.

                        WARD
No, it needs to be said. A real man takes a chance. A real man stands up for something, makes a mark on this world. When the chips are on the table, cards are down, you need to take a number, be counted. Tough times, those are when . . . what you do *defines* you. You can take a stand, or you can fold up in a little ball, afraid to even try. Just be another nobody, forgotten soon as you're gone. (*beat; in SAM's face*) No sir. I ain't a loser. I grab the cow by the horns. (*beat; to all:*) This is going to make us rich. Mark my words.

BLACKOUT

Scene 6

(RITA walks into spotlight, downstage center. Nothing else is lit.)

The preceding was brought to you by Java Hut's Decaffeinated Instant Crystals, the best instant coffee on the planet, without any of the caffeine. Java Hut's Crystals use only the finest in real coffee beans, hand-picked and ground in the Java Hut, run by Mr. Java himself, a kindly old man with a mustache and a limp, living on a quiet hillside somewhere in the country where it never rains and animals run free.

The caffeine is removed by a secret, patented process that I can't divulge here. The grounds are freeze-dried and vacuum-packed and freeze-packed and vacuum-dried, ready for your cup and guaranteed to give you no jitters whatsoever, mild enough to drink before going to bed or bottle-feed your newborn baby, not capable at all of WAKING YOU UP.

Java Hut's Decaffeinated Crystals are . . . (*pause, looks at product, drops voice*) well, I don't know if it's really "the best on the planet." How do they make coffee instant anyway? It's not like a coffee maker is that difficult to deal with. And I'm not sure the reasoning behind taking the caffeine out. I thought that was why everyone drank it. And these beans were probably picked somewhere in Africa, using local children recruited into those coffee armies and forced to shoot their friends and family . . . oh, maybe that's diamonds. No, coffee is the one that recruits poor Latin children to pick the beans until their fingers bleed and pays them seven cents a year, I think. Something like that.

I do know that the good news is coffee is now good for you. I read it the other day. It used to be bad for you, all that acid in your stomach, something about cancer and tumors and the like, but now it's good for you, just like chocolate. It's good for your heart. And . . . (*squinting toward audience as if reading a cue card*) and it helps you lose height. No, I'm sorry, that's "weight." I think. And lowers cholesterol. And helps men grow hair and last longer in bed and gives them very pronounced abs and firmer erections. (*conspiratorially, toward audience*) *Very* pronounced abs. And I hear it was used as a truth serum during World War II! (*Pause.*) Excuse me? Oh, OK. I'm sorry. Yes, less editorializing. Sure, I'll work on that. Next time.

BLACKOUT

Scene 7

(Later that evening. Low light. SAM sits cross-legged on a couch cushion on the living room floor, attempting to meditate. Wind blows periodically, activating chimes. After a few beats, a dog barks. Then again. Sam shifts slightly, keeping his eyes closed. A cat meows. SAM sighs. Dog barks again, sustained.)

SAM (hushed)
Shut up!
(Silence. SAM relaxes again. After a few beats, all at the same time, wind chimes sound, a dog barks, a cat meows, a rooster crows, general chaos.)
Shut up!
(Silence for a few beats. Then, softly at first but growing louder, the sound of murmuring voices, followed by the slithering and stomping, and finally, Sam's heartbeat. The volume builds until it sounds as if a beast has approached the house and waits just outside the front door.

SAM is terrified. From his bag in the corner he pulls out his headphones and puts them on. This dulls the sound of everything but his heartbeat.

A moment of silence, followed by a pounding at the door. SAM hurriedly pulls a uniform from his bag and puts it on; it's the "T" superhero outfit we saw him wearing in the first scene. He wraps his arms around himself for protection. The sounds, other than his heartbeat, are halted.

Looking for distraction, he pulls his laptop out of his backpack and turns it on. Light from the laptop shines brightly, but the screen faces away from audience.

From the dark hallway appears MEREDITH, dressed in the gown resembling a comic-book princess with ears of corn randomly attached. She appears to be glowing slightly, as if wrapped in Christmas lights. She wears a tiara, perhaps lit. For the first half of this scene she speaks with an almost regal, somewhat lightheaded tone, not unlike Gilda, the Good Witch of the East.)

SAM

Meredith.

MEREDITH

Oh. Greetings, Sam, what a surprise. (beat) How are you?

(SAM doesn't hear at first, then removes headphones from ears.)

SAM

Just fine. I'm doing fine.

MEREDITH

Of course you are, my poor, sweet Sam.

SAM

So. The universe taking care of you OK?

MEREDITH

I can't complain.

SAM

I'm sure you can with a little effort. (beat) I should've told you this when I had the chance, but I never liked the way you chewed your food.

MEREDITH

I see. You know of course you're just trying to make yourself feel better.

SAM

And that. I hate that. You were always telling me what I'm thinking or what I'm trying to say.

MEREDITH

We both know you don't really mean that.

(Pause.)

SAM
I need to ask you something, Meredith.

MEREDITH
I'm all ears.

SAM
I just don't understand: why?

MEREDITH
Why what, Sam?

SAM
Why all of this? Why did you leave?

MEREDITH
Why did I leave?

SAM
Will you please stop repeating everything I say. Yes, why did you leave. Why all the affairs. Why the lies.

MEREDITH
Yes. Well. I'm not proud of my behavior . . . But I'm not sure you'd understand.

SAM
Try me. (beat) I was under the impression we were happy.

MEREDITH
I'm afraid you misinterpreted.

SAM
Then why were we together in the first place?

MEREDITH
(with growing theatricality)
Why. Sam, why are leaves green? Why do lions hunt the antelope? Why does the tide obey the whims of the moon? It's our nature, Sam. Our instinct. We must obey or live an incomplete life. You didn't really listen to your instinct. You didn't follow anything but the script.

SAM
Oh please. I'm normal. I believe people get married, buy a house, have kids, earn increasingly higher salaries, try to retire early and see the Grand Canyon in the summer.

MEREDITH (singing)
(singing)
". . . and a partridge in a pear tree."

SAM
No matter how you try to rationalize, I refuse to believe infidelity is anyone's nature.

MEREDITH
Passion, Sam. It's passion. We all have it, it's just that not everyone embraces it, allows it to breathe. To ignore my passion is to stop my heart from beating. If I were to mute that fierce internal wail, I'd be numb. Unfeeling, unresponsive. I'd sleepwalk numbly through my days. I'd be like the undead, like a mummy.

SAM
Zombie.

MEREDITH
Mummy, zombie . . .

SAM
When people talk of "following their passion," they're usually referring to an art form or vocation. I don't think it applies to nymphomania.

MEREDITH (defensively)
I'm a spiritual being! I'm always seeking to transcend the physical. I've sought out my spirit animal. I regularly dream that I frolic with horses!

SAM
You frolic with—

MEREDITH
The point is, we cannot ignore our true nature and still lead a fulfilling life. You have to run through the woods beside your animal self; dance naked your primal tango. Otherwise it's just too . . . boring. (beat) Look, Sam, you spend all your time pouring coffee and making small talk with customers, counting change and pondering . . . biscotti. You come home every night smelling of hazelnut and espresso. And that's fine except . . . except that it's fine. For you. And nothing will ever change. You won't let it.

SAM
You don't know that.

MEREDITH
Yes. I do. The truth is, our lives are nothing but change, Sam; nothing stays the same for a second. The cells in our bodies, the weather, the cars we drive, everything is constantly changing, moving in some direction. Trying to control any of it, even just trying to stand still . . . It goes against our nature. And it just makes you miserable.

SAM (meekly)

There's nothing wrong with a little consistency. You didn't used to mind it.

MEREDITH

I changed. Things change. Life is not consistent.

(Pause.)

SAM

Our last anniversary, at that Italian restaurant. You were in the bathroom for a long time and our waiter disappeared. You didn't by any chance . . .

MEREDITH

My memory, Sam . . . I'm not very good with details.

SAM

We were happy at one time, weren't we? In the beginning?

MEREDITH

(quietly conceding)
For a while.

(Pause.)

SAM

And your taste in music. That airy, ethereal keyboard nonsense. I never liked it. (beat) But now the house is so quiet. And I'm hearing things. Things that might've been there the whole time and I never noticed.

MEREDITH

I'm sure it's just stress, Sam. Try drinking more. (beat) You just need to start moving on, Sam.

SAM

I don't know how.

(Pause. Offstage, a horse whinnies.)

MEREDITH

I have to go, Sam, my ride's here. (beat) Take care of yourself, Sam. Really.

(MEREDITH turns with a flourish as her spotlight and tiara go dark. SAM closes laptop and puts his head down on computer.)

BLACKOUT

Scene 8

(Later. CHLOE and SAM sitting downstage in a circle of light.) He still wears the bathrobe he's been in since the beginning.

SAM
Just to make sure: none of this conversation will actually be seen by anyone, right? I mean, we're just talking.

CHLOE
Of course, Sam. It's just you and me. (beat) So. You own a coffee shop. How did that come about?

SAM
I used to work there, for the previous owner. Actually started back in high school part time. Hung out there so much that I finally just ended up behind the counter. (beat) Nobody ever came in though. He'd put mannequins in the barstools to make it look like we had customers.

CHLOE
Resourceful.

SAM
But he ran it into the ground, always trying new gimmicks. If you keep changing things you just chase people away. Customers want consistency.

CHLOE
Good, solid business sense.

SAM
I have my regulars, folks I see nearly every evening after a hard day. For them it's a sanctuary. An escape. No matter what goes on in the outside world, in my cafe they're always somebody.

CHLOE
Seems like you enjoy your work.

SAM
Maybe it's not significant to most folks but I think I serve a purpose. Though I'm taking a little time off for now.

CHLOE
Oh, yes, on account of the recent jilting. It's only been a little under a month, am I right?

SAM
Jilting? I don't—

CHLOE
Tell me about her. Your wife. Ex-wife. Estranged.

SAM
I'm not sure I really feel comfortable.

CHLOE
Viewers are going to want to know. It's backstory, sweetie, we're doing this with all of you. Helps explain who you are. In this case maybe it helps us understand, why, for instance, you look like a zombie and you're still wearing a bathrobe.

SAM
OK. Well, she was—is—very attractive.

CHLOE (bitterly)
Always the bottom line with men, isn't it? The looks? That's what really matters, isn't it? Long as your breasts are perky and butt tight, it's all peaches and vodka. Once they start getting just a little bit—

                            SAM
Excuse me?

                            CHLOE
What?

                            SAM
She left me.

                            CHLOE
Right, sorry. Well, I'm sure your income was a factor.

                            SAM
My income?

                            CHLOE
     (zipping lip)
Forget I said anything. We want to hear from you. Where were we? Right, your wife. Attractive, nice figure, yadda yadda.

                            SAM
Sure, you could say—

CHLOE
Long hair? Short?

                            SAM
About down to here. Green eyes. Dimples when she squints or smiles. She did this thing with her hair—

                            CHLOE
     (to offstage)
Cody, make a note, see if Renee is available. Or that one we used in the commercial, with curly hair.

[Note: she should describe the actress playing MEREDITH as closely as possible.]

SAM

What are you talking about?

CHLOE

Casting. Just in case. Nothing definite, we just want to cover our bases.
    (SAM is perplexed but CHLOE moves on.)
Tell me . . . how did you two meet?

SAM

We met online. In a virtual cafe.

CHLOE

Really.

SAM

I've always preferred virtual socialization to the real thing. It's quieter.

CHLOE

Yet you run a coffee shop.

SAM

It's different. See, in the cafe I'm the owner. I'm working, fulfilling a role. Online, meeting someone virtually, I can be myself.

CHLOE

So that's where you're more you.

SAM

Exactly. No expectation, no roles. It's straightforward. Just two people talking. Well, typing.

CHLOE
So an online cafe. Lemme guess: you drink virtual coffee?

SAM
In a way. It's like a projected identity. An image of how you want others to see you. (beat) Meredith was a goddess.

CHLOE
We've gone from 'attractive' to 'goddess.'

SAM (admiringly)
No, her avatar. Called herself the Corn Goddess. Had a long robe, tiara made of vines, the whole bit. She glowed.

CHLOE (skeptically)
Uh-huh. And what were you? Wait, lemme guess: a knight.

SAM
Oh please. That's so cliché. (beat) I was a superhero.

CHLOE
A superhero.

SAM
Terrapin Man. Impenetrable shell, immeasurable strength. Little slow, but still.

CHLOE
Turtle. Right.

SAM
Terrapin, actually. Common mistake. They actually don't belong to the sea turtle family. Terrapins specifically live in brackish water.

CHLOE
Fascinating—

                              SAM

Americans say "turtle" to refer to freshwater species as well
as the land-dwellers. British have a completely different
system. Seems the poor terrapin's identity is really just a
matter of perspective.

                             CHLOE

That a fact.

                              SAM

In some folklore, terrapins are considered sacred and believed
to host powerful water spirits. It is considered extremely bad
luck to harm a terrapin. (beat) Extremely bad luck.

                             CHLOE

So. Presenting yourself as a human-sized sea—excuse me,
brackish water—creature and typing on a computer seems
more authentic to you than meeting someone in person.

                              SAM

I know it might sound strange, but yes, in a way.

                             CHLOE

Didn't you ever worry that you're actually communicating
with a sweaty shirtless man wearing a dog collar and coated in
Vaseline?

                              SAM

These rooms do involve a certain level of trust. But do you
think meeting someone in person makes it any more truthful?

                             CHLOE

Well for starters, at least you know their gender. (beat) In
most cases, anyway.

SAM
I think it's a lot easier to be honest with people when the facade is obvious. It's liberating. (beat) But look, it was just a hobby. It wasn't who I am. I mean, I wasn't one of those guys.

CHLOE
Those guys?

SAM
The geeks. Those obsessed guys who spend all day on a keyboard and make arcane science fiction references. (beat) I mean I don't actually think I'm a terrapin in real life.

CHLOE
Not a terrapin. I'll make a note of that.

(CHLOE writes in notebook.)

SAM
Let me ask you something.

CHLOE
Go right ahead.

SAM
When it's quiet, when you think it's completely silent . . . what do you hear?

CHLOE
I don't think I understand you.

SAM
Have you ever experienced complete silence?

CHLOE
Lord no. That sounds terrifying. Is there even such a thing?

(SAM nods.)

CHLOE

That's what you wanted to ask? If I've ever experienced silence?

SAM

That's all.

CHLOE

You're a strange creature, Sam. (beat) OK . . . So tell me before we wrap up . . . Give me a quick snapshot of who you are. Boil it down for me.

SAM

What do you mean.

CHLOE

What viewers will want to know is this: Who is the real you? Underneath it all? In as few words as possible.

SAM

Who am I? How should I know?

CHLOE

For the viewers, Sam.

SAM (exasperated)

Who am I? OK, I'm that guy. I'm the husband whose wife left him. The business owner who can't afford his mortgage and still took a leave of absence. (beat) The prodigal son returned home to the scene of repeated crimes. The 'late bloomer' who will most likely never actually bloom.

I was the smart kid with so much potential who just needed a good swift kick in the pants. The one who never learned to take life by the horns, never really figured out what this dream is that he's supposed to follow, the guy whose name rings a bell but you just can't place the face.

I'm the guy in the back of the photo, a little out of focus and half-cropped out of the frame. (beat) I'm all of those guys. The one who never really wins, who makes you feel better about not being him. I'm the loser. I'm the audience. I'm everyone but the hero.

Who am I? You tell me.

BLACKOUT

END OF ACT

ACT II

Scene 1

(Morning. The house has been cleaned up, lights are bright. Music should shift to a canned, brassy sound as curtain rises.

WARD and RITA will articulate deliberately, aware they're on camera; SARA is generally annoyed. Everyone still wears name tags, and will continue to do so throughout.)

WARD (entering)

Honey, I'm home.

(RITA comes onto landing at the top of the stairs.)

RITA

Buongiorno, dear.
(WARD makes "hushing" motions with hands.)
What?

WARD (surrendering)

Never mind.

RITA

How was the fishing today?

WARD

Not good. As usual, the independent fisherman is being squeezed by special interest groups, government regulations, and inaccurate research. Soon, America's oldest industry could be a thing of the past.

RITA

Oh, that's wonderful, dear. (beat) Can I make you something good to eat?

                    WARD
Why yes. I would love something good to eat.

   (They both enter kitchen.)

                    WARD
It's very cold outside. And the wind is blowing hard.

                    RITA
Sounds as if the weather is quite . . . forlorn.

   (WARD sits at table. RITA rummages in cupboards.)

                    RITA
How about some soup? We have both canned and instant.

                    WARD
Canned will be fine.

                    RITA
And some pie.

   (WARD is alarmed, and attempts to subtly wave his arms to cancel the pie.)

                    RITA
   (interpreting)
Or . . . not . . . no. No pie.
   (deliberately)
We do not have any pie.

   (WARD gives up, head in hands.)

                    WARD
Where are our children?

RITA
Loro sono andati al negozio: They went to the store. They should be back any moment.

(Pause. SARA enters while knocking, followed by SAM.)

WARD
Why look, it's our only daughter, Sara. And her brother, Sam.

RITA
Hello, children.

(SAM and SARA appear a little confused by their reaction.)

SARA
Well you two sound natural.

WARD (loudly)
Why did you go shopping? We have food. We're not starving you know. Though soon you might not be able to buy fresh fish from fishermen.

SARA
Sam needed fresh vegetables.

SAM
Mom, you should be eating less processed food.

(Pause. RITA is confused, WARD is discouraged because the show is not going according to plan.)

RITA
Processed food?

                    WARD
Long as you don't start smoking marijuana in the house.
That's the next thing isn't it?

   (SAM and SARA look confused.)

                    SARA (sarcastically)
Actually, that might help with the contest, don't you think?
Rampant drug use, maybe heroin. Or a sex addiction.

                    WARD
What contest? I don't know what you mean.

                    SAM
Good one.

                    SARA
We could get a little more sensationalistic. Folks love that
crap.

                    SAM
As a matter of fact, I have been meaning to ask—
    (mimicking WARD's speech)
Sara, have you been impregnated by anyone at work lately?

                    SARA
Not since the last time. But that was before I became a
lesbian love slave.

                    RITA
Sara, per favore.

                    SARA
   (to SAM)
And you? Have you had unprotected sex with any prostitutes
today?

SAM
Nope, just with myself, but thanks for asking.

WARD
(breaking character)
That's enough outta both of you!

(CHLOE enters from offstage followed by CODY, carrying a camera.)

CHLOE
OK, OK, cut. This isn't working for me.
(to SAM and SARA)
You two are way too stiff.

SARA
We're too stiff?

CODY
(to SARA)
I thought you were just great.

SARA
Thank you.

(She begins to look at CODY with curiosity.)

CHLOE
(to SARA)
Look, we can't be talking about this as a show.

SARA
But it is a show.

CHLOE
No, that's where you're wrong. It's reality.

SARA

(deliberately)
No . . . it's television.

CHLOE (patronizingly)
Look, deep down, people just want to believe. They don't want to hear that they're watching a TV show, that it's not "real," or they're "wasting their time." This (motioning around to set) is all that matters. This is the "real." There's nothing outside of this real, got it?

RITA

(to WARD)
Ward, I don't understand what this woman is saying.

CHLOE
We just need to keep it contained. No outside references, there's nothing out there, understand? You might as well be talking about Martians, or . . . Canada.

SAM
But it is a television program. And Canada—

CHLOE
You know that, I know that . . . Look, I'm just offering some gentle guidance. I mean, we can't have you just roaming around, babbling, can we? (beat) Matter of fact, we should probably give you some lines to work on.

RITA
Lines? Like a script?

CHLOE
Not exactly. More general. Nothing major. And don't forget to hold products up a little higher. Like the soup can. We need to really push those endorsements. (beat) OK everyone, so take five. (beat) That means take a break.

(Pause. All relax. CHLOE turns to CODY.)
How'd I look?

                        CODY

Fine.

                       CHLOE

Through the camera. Look through the camera.

(CODY raises camera as CHLOE adjusts hair, etc.)

                        CODY

Fine.

                       CHLOE

Fine? I want to look great. Fantastic. Tell me I look amazing.

                        CODY

You look amazing.

                       CHLOE

You bet I do. I am one sexy bitch. I'd do me. (beat) That camera just loves me.

(CODY walks downstage and addresses audience.)

                CODY (enthusiastically)

And this isn't just any camera, Chloe, it's a Konvas 1M, the model favored by Andrei Tarkovsky, featuring a three-prime-lens turret design with lightweight glass for easier portability. Switching from wide to normal and telephoto is a breeze, and the smaller lenses are great in dim light. Plus, the anamorphic optics increase resolution by more than fifty percent.

                       CHLOE

That's great, Cody!

CODY

Thanks, Chloe. Now, I know what you're thinking: why is he using film? That's so old-fashioned. Why isn't he shooting digital? I'll give you one reason: posterity. With digital, you're always one hard-drive crash away from losing your footage, while properly stored film can last for hundreds of years without losing integrity. Want another reason? Flexibility. You can print from film or export to digital or high-def in a snap. But the most important reason of all? Reality. Upgrades in film have made shooting in 35 millimeter richer than ever. The truth is 35 millimeter gives you an honest image quality that's even better than the real thing: with 35 millimeter, you're not shooting life, you're shooting art.

(CODY smiles for a beat and returns to his previous pose, ready to film CHOLE, who again primps for the camera.)

CHLOE

And . . . cut.

BLACKOUT

Scene 2

(Later that afternoon. SAM and SARA sit at the kitchen table playing Quarters with coffee, taking turns bouncing a quarter into a third cup on the table. When one makes a shot, the other drinks; when one misses, the other shoots.

Both are obviously wired on caffeine. Throughout the scene they're speaking will become comically faster and more intense.)

SAM

(makes his shot)
Another one. Drink.
(SARA does so, then fills her mug up with more coffee.)
So in general you see no greater plan to the universe. No organization whatsoever.

SARA

I never said that. What I was saying is that I don't believe in a deity's greater plan. "God's grand design" and all that. Just because we haven't figured everything out yet doesn't mean it can't be explained rationally.

SAM

Though some would say that's exactly when faith is most necessary. When we don't understand something, we just have to trust that it's part of a plan.

SARA

But that's a total copout.

SAM

How so?

SARA

"Well, I don't understand why I'm here so I'm just going to go with what the well-dressed man in front of the congregation tells me to do because he seems so self-assured." Whatever.

SAM

Works for a lot of folks.

SARA

People are just afraid of what they don't know. And then there are those who have a very difficult time admitting they don't know something. Either way. God's just an excuse.

(Pause.)

SAM

Let me ask you something: When everything's quiet, do you hear anything?

SARA

What?

SAM

When there's no noise and everything's silent, what do you hear?

SARA

That's the same thing you asked Mom. It doesn't make any sense.

SAM

Why not?

SARA

Because it's quiet, moron. Like Mom said: quiet is quiet. It's like asking what you see in the dark.

SAM

So? What do you see in the dark?

SARA
You know what I mean, freak. It's quiet for chrissake.

SAM
So when it's quiet, you hear nothing.

SARA
When you don't speak, I don't hear you. Yeah.

SAM
What about shells?

SARA
What about what?

SAM
Shells. Sea shells. They're quiet, right? I mean, nothing going on inside. Yet when you hold them up to your ear, you hear the sea.

SARA
Right, well, I'm sure that's subjective. Mom probably hears a church organ.

SAM
That's not very nice.

SARA
Wish there was a way we could find out. Why don't you put your ear up to hers and see if you can hear anything.

SAM
I had a serious question.

SARA
It's a stupid question.

SAM

Why is it stupid?

SARA

Because, doofus, if there's nothing to hear, I'm not going to hear anything.

SAM

Well, yeah, sure, literally, but I'm—

SARA

How fast you move when you're standing still? What do you smell when your nose is plugged? What's the sound of one freakin' hand clapping (demonstrating)?

SAM

Yeah, OK. I get it.

SARA

Pointless.

SAM

Yeah, OK. Forget it.

(Pause.)

SARA (calmer)

One of our tenants at the shelter is a vet. We call him the General but I don't think he ever really was. Anyway, he told me something once.

SAM

About?

SARA

He was in a sensory deprivation tank once. In the army. Some sort of experiment I guess.

SAM
What'd he say about it?

SARA
That he could see why people go crazy in there. There's nothing but you.

SAM
Really.

SARA
Can't imagine myself.

SAM
Did he say what he sounded like?

SARA (relenting)
He said you hear things you never hear. Sounds of the body going throughout its day, I guess. Weird sounds: gurgling, sloshing. Heart beating like thunder. Then you start hearing other things, he said.

SAM
What other things?

SARA
He wouldn't say, just that he wasn't sure if they were real or not. Guess it's kind of impossible to tell.

(Pause.)
SAM
What if what you're hearing is you? I mean, there's nothing else. You're just hearing your self.

                    SARA
Whatever it is it's enough to drive people crazy. At least in the movies. (beat) So why the interest in sounds? You making a really annoying CD or something?

                    SAM
I'm just trying to figure some things out.

   (Pause.)
                    SARA
When I first quit drinking, I had no idea what to do with my time. I didn't know what regular people did. Go on a date? Are you kidding me? My plans had always revolved around how I'd be numbing myself that day, nothing else. Then when I stopped, I felt like I'd been dropped in a foreign country without a map. (beat) I think sobriety was the first time I've ever really felt alone.

   (Pause.)

                    SAM
Do you think they're happy?

                    SARA
Who?

                    SAM
Mom and Dad.

              SARA (considering)
I don't know. I suppose so, in some bizarre way.

                    SAM
Could just be habit.

                    SARA
It could.

(WARD enters through front door carrying mail. He puts down all but one letter and opens it.)

SARA

Well, hello.

(WARD doesn't hear. He pulls out the letter, which is on colored paper. He reads it and deflates, then sets it down on the kitchen table. He pours himself a drink, knocks it back, and pours another, then sits at table.)

SARA

Starting a little early don't ya think?

WARD

You're the expert.

(SARA is visibly, if only momentarily, hurt.)

SAM

Jesus Dad, what's that supposed to mean?

WARD

Means I will not be questioned in my own house, that's what it means.

(Pause.)

SAM

Is that bad news?

WARD

What?

SAM

The letter. Is it bad?

WARD

Well it ain't good.

(CHLOE and CODY enter from offstage. WARD has no reaction. SAM and SARA have both forgotten about them.)

SARA

You were filming us the whole time? Isn't there some warning you can give when we're on camera?

CHLOE

That would sort of ruin the fun, wouldn't it? But I wouldn't be too concerned, not much of this is usable. Not enough jazz. Not catchy enough. There's no plan, you're just talking. Opening mail.

SARA

You mean like real people.

CHLOE

Listen, this is supposed to be reality television. We're not interested in what "real people" would do. We want drama. Excitement. Controversy. You give us that, and you folks get on TV. And the audience gets to live vicariously through your experience. Everybody wins.

WARD

(to CHLOE)
Lemme ask you something. When are we gonna see the money?

CHLOE

What money.

WARD
The ten thousand dollars we're supposed to get for doing this. I thought we'd get paid up front.

CHLOE
We've already addressed that.

RITA (O.S.)
Ward, is that you?

WARD
No, we didn't address it.

CHLOE
I already told you, the money is for one family, the one that ends up on the show. It's not for each finalist.

(Pause. CHLOE is losing patience; WARD is still confused, unwilling to accept this despite knowing it's true.)

RITA
(on landing)
Ward?

WARD
Yes, I'm here, goddammit.

SARA
(admonishing)
Dad.

RITA
(to WARD)
You don't need to snap at me.

WARD
(to CHLOE)

I think something's suspicious here. The paper promised ten thousand dollars.

                    CODY
I'm afraid you read that incorrectly, dude. You'll get the money if you're chosen. Only the final family earns the reward.

                    CHLOE (dismissively)
Like I said, we've been through this.

                    WARD (frustrated)
Some of us have bills to pay. Debts.

                    CHLOE
     (ignoring WARD; thinking hard)
There's just no hook here.

                    SAM
What do you mean "hook?"

                    CHLOE
Nothing grabs me.

                    SARA
We're a fishing family. How can we not have a hook?

   (SAM gives her pained look. SARA shrugs.)

                    CODY (sarcastically)
Maybe they could sing and dance.

                    WARD
This isn't right.

   (WARD sulks at kitchen table with bottle.)

SARA
(to CODY, joining joke)
You know, I like it. We could make this into a musical.

CHLOE (sarcastically)
Yes, Cody, that's a brilliant idea. (beat) Maybe a love interest or something.

SARA
No, seriously. You know how people in musicals just spontaneously break into song? Would that be a better way to go?

CODY
If you can sing, maybe.

SARA
Look at Mom up there, like she's on a balcony. Wouldn't this be a good time for a song?
  (to RITA)
Mom, give us a tune.

RITA
Well I . . . I always did love musicals.

SARA
Not too peppy, but not a downer either.

CODY
More Webber than Sondheim.

SAM (enthusiastically)
Or like those annoying movies where a group of older women spontaneously lurch into a choreographed routine they all somehow know. Maybe we could do one of those numbers, what do you think?

SARA
Yeah, well, maybe not that.

CODY
But the musical idea I kinda like.

CHLOE (awakening)
What? Are you high?

CODY
Right now?

CHLOE
A musical? I don't think so.

SAM
Would certainly get people's attention.

CHLOE
Musicals are ridiculous. No one sings in real life.

SARA
Well maybe they should. It's not like we're suggesting a cartoon.

(RITA comes downstairs.)

RITA (enthusiastically)
Sara, are we doing a musical now?

CHLOE
Forget it. How many times have I told you: this is reality television. We have to look real, only more interesting. (beat) I'm thinking maybe the love interest.

SARA
A love interest.

CHLOE
Of some sort. Maybe we could find Sam's ex.

SAM
Hold on, I don't think so.

CHLOE
Would bring some drama.

SAM
She's got nothing to do with this.

CHLOE
We have to give the audience something they can identify with, something familiar, then make it slightly less empty than their actual lives. Vicarious fulfillment: That's what this is all about. Otherwise nobody watches.

SARA
And we can't have that.

CHLOE
Of course not. It would kill the show. And television is my life.

(RITA slowly walks downstage.)

RITA
I was in one in high school you know. A musical. I wasn't the lead, but—

SARA
(to CHLOE)
And without the show, lord knows what people would do with their time.

CHLOE

(to SARA)
They'd watch something else. And yours truly would be back on the nightly news, standing on a rainy street, reporting about the latest local fundraiser with hair like a Chia pet.

RITA

My part was big enough. I had one song almost all to myself.

SARA

(to CHLOE)
So realistic it is. We wouldn't want to mislead viewers in any way.

CHLOE

(to SARA)
Absolutely. Now you're getting it. (beat) If we agree on the definition of "misleading."

RITA

But I got sick the night before we opened and another girl got the part.

CODY

I still vote for the musical.

CHLOE

Well, I'm sorry, but I don't recall asking you.

RITA

But I always wanted to have one chance.
(RITA, having arrived at the edge of the stage, begins singing.)
"The hills are alive . . ."

CHLOE

What the hell do you think you're doing?

                    RITA
(singing)
"With the sound of music . . ."

                    CHLOE
Please stop.

                    RITA
(singing)
"With songs they have sung for a thousand years."

(Music and singing suddenly stops as WARD smashes a chair over the table. Everyone freezes.)

                    WARD
(slowly and intensely)
This is not a game. This is my life!

BLACKOUT

Scene 3

(Later that evening. Chair is still smashed in kitchen, laptop in pieces in living room. Everyone will act more wary of WARD, who is getting increasingly drunk.

CHLOE stares into camera, held by CODY. She wears a flashy, revealing outfit.)

CHLOE

How do I look?

CODY

Fine.

CHLOE

Fine? Just fine?

CODY

(lacking enthusiasm)
Great. Fabulous. Ravishing.

CHLOE

You're damn right I do. I look fantastic.

CODY

Of course you do.

CHLOE

My god I'm sexy. Look at me. Look at me!

CODY

(activating camera)
OK, we're rolling—

CHLOE

Welcome back to "All the World's a Stage." Today we're continuing our series that uncovers the everyday life of a family unit disintegrating under the pressure of a dying lifestyle. In this case, it's a fishing family, featuring an aging fisherman, financially desperate as his industry crumbles, accompanied by his supportive but not-particularly-alert wife, along with their two children: a recently widowed son with a possible drug problem and his sister, a repressed lesbian. Let's tune in . . .

(CHLOE and CODY move offstage, downstage left. Drum roll and brassy, cheesy music. WARD and RITA enter at the top of the stairs. RITA wears a dress and apron reminiscent of Aunt Bee. WARD, becoming progressively bitterer, wears a fisherman's bib over a sweatshirt, with matching rubber boots. He looks in the direction of CHLOE's exit.)

WARD
What did she mean "dying lifestyle?"

RITA
I haven't seen you in your fishing gear in a long time. It looks good.

(They come downstairs.)

WARD
I don't know what's going on here. "Dying lifestyle." What if it is? What the hell's her point?

(SAM and SARA enter from door. SAM wears a sporty black suit with an open collar and grease in his hair. Again he wears headphones. He is a little more agitated and distracted than he was before. SARA, following, wears the exact same outfit CHLOE wore, and is just as made up. She is clearly uncomfortable with the look.)

SARA

I feel like an idiot in this.

SAM (loudly)

You? I feel like a coke dealer.

RITA

Oh, Sam, you look so handsome.

SAM

(not hearing her)
What?!
(CHLOE AND CODY, with camera, enter as WARD pours himself a drink, knocks it back, pours another and puts the bottle on table.)

CHLOE

Whoa, whoa, whoa. What are these?
(SARA raps her knuckles on SAM's headphones.)
We can't have unauthorized wardrobe changes.

SAM

Do I have to take them off?

CHLOE

I'm afraid so.

SAM

I don't feel very comfortable with this arrangement.

CHLOE

You don't have to be comfortable.

WARD (disgusted)

I'm starting to wonder if we're being had. I'm starting to think this whole thing's a charade.

SARA
(to WARD)
Now you're getting suspicious? What tipped you off, the fact that we're all pretending to be people we're not?

WARD
Just getting the feeling this might be rigged from the start. Something's smelling a little fishy here.

SARA
(to WARD)
Seriously? "Fishy?"

CHLOE
Nothing's rigged. This is television for chrissake. And we're rolling.

RITA
Who's wants some tea? Sam?

SARA
Mom, if you make it, we will drink.

WARD (sourly)
Why don't you go ahead and have some pie while you're at it. What the hell, let's all have some pie.

RITA
Well, all right Ward, I'll heat some up.

WARD
(to SARA, just noticing her look)
What's your story?

SARA
What do you mean?

                              WARD
You look different.

                              SARA
Oh, that's because I've become a prostitute.

    (CHLOE approaches with CODY in tow.)

                              CHLOE
Cut, cut. No, this won't do at all.

                              RITA
Mama mia.

                              CHLOE
    (to SARA)
"Prostitute?"

                              SARA
"Repressed lesbian?"

                              RITA
    (to CHLOE)
Would you like some tea?

                              CHLOE
People, people. Work with me, work with me.

                              SARA
    (to SAM)
Did she actually say that?

                              CHLOE
I'm trying to make you stars. (beat; patiently) Look, if you just follow the outline we talked about, and make it sound natural, you'll do fine. None of this freelancing. Don't try to follow your own instincts—you have no instincts. Just act your

parts. OK? Are we on the same page? (beat) Good. Just trust me. I'm a professional.

SARA

A professional what?

(CODY laughs.)

CHLOE
(to CODY)
Oh, you think that's funny? How'd you like another assignment at the old folks' home?
(to SARA)
I've worked with difficult actors before, but you're pushing it.

SARA
(to CHLOE)
I am not an actress!

CHLOE
Look, either toe the line, or stay off the porch.

SARA (confused)

What?

CHLOE
OK, let's not make this a complete waste of time. Up to now, I have seen worse. Maybe. Nothing I've worked on of course, but I'm sure people have been worse. So this time, let's put a little more feeling into it. More drama.

SARA
Look, we've been doing this nonstop since yesterday. Why don't we just take a break?

RITA
We're exhausted. You even filmed us in our sleep.

SARA
(to RITA)
Really? That's very creepy.

CHLOE
Look folks, I don't know who told you this was easy, but they were wrong. It's hard work, presenting yourself, creating your identity. You can't just stop when you want.

SARA (sarcastically)
Got to keep on the faces for the faces that you'll meet.

CHLOE
Lemme tell you something. I've interviewed politicians, I've interviewed athletes, I've interviewed recording artists. Anyone who's done anything in this town, I was there to observe it, firsthand. Without me no one would know they even existed. I gave them their talent.

SAM
What?

CHLOE
If a tree falls in the forest . . . ?

SARA
It's still a tree?

CHLOE
Point being, talent doesn't exist until someone says it does. Someone like me. I bestow celebrity. I define status. I give life.
   (Lights dim as CHLOE moves toward edge of stage and into a spotlight. She speaks out over the audience with excessive conviction. Perhaps "My Way" crescendos in background.)

I was once where you are. In your shoes. I was a nobody, just trying to make it. Struggling through auditions, trying to find an agent, mingling with the regular people. (distastefully) The "service industry."

Then I realized that to really make it, you have to become someone else. You have to be whoever people want you to be, even when they don't know who they want. You see, it's not about finding out who you really are; it's all about finding out who you can make yourself into. (beat) Yes, there were times I'm sure you knew, when I bit off more than I could chew, but through it all, when there was doubt, (louder) I ate it up and spit it out. (singing loudly) I faced it all and I stood tall, and did it my way!

                    WARD

Jesus Christ!

   (SARA looks at CODY, who shrugs. CHLOE and CODY leave stage as before.)

                    CHLOE

(O.S.)
OK, let's make some reality! And . . . action!

                BLACKOUT

Scene 4

(RITA walks into a spotlight holding product; rest of stage is dark.)

"A Full Night's Sheep, the safest sleep aid on the market, guaranteed to put you right to sleep as safely as counting sheep, only deeper, and with no harmful side effects."
    (breaks character)
"Put you to sleep as safely as counting sheep." I think they should change that, it's very difficult to say. (beat) But don't we have enough of these things? So many sleep aids out there, each saying it induces a stronger coma. (beat) Every day I see commercials for stuff I don't care about: trucks, perfume, allergy medicine . . . they're all telling me I want these things, but I don't. I don't care. I just want to sit and watch the stars come out at night and sip a cup of tea. I just want to smell smoke coming from chimneys in the winter. And see smiles on the faces of family. These are the things I really like. Things I can really experience. And I don't think you can bottle those.
    (looks at package)
I don't want to sleep more.
    (listens for a beat toward audience, then sighs)
Yes, I understand: I'm going off script again. Fine. (beat) You know, after this is over, I don't think I want to do it anymore.

BLACKOUT

Scene 5

(SARA, SAM, WARD and RITA are mutely arguing and gesticulating on one side of stage while CODY and CHLOE watch from the other.)

CHLOE
This is ridiculous. Look at them.
   (Pause.)
Amateurs.

CODY
I think Sara's pretty cute.
   (CHLOE snorts.)
They have been at it for a while.
   (Pause. CHLOE is not persuaded.)
I could use a break myself.

CHLOE
They just don't matter. These people are just like everybody else. Living their lives . . . just . . . suffering. Everybody suffers. We don't want to watch it.

CODY
I thought the point was to a family audiences could relate to.

CHLOE
People don't want to see themselves. They want either to see someone they wish they could be, or someone they're glad not to be — the rich pop star or the broke train wreck, nothing in between. Craving or aversion, that's what it's all about. That's life.

CODY
   (skeptically)
Just that simple.

CHLOE
It all comes down those to two things: craving or aversion. Anything else and you and I are out of work.

(Pause.)

CODY
So have you heard anything?

CHLOE
About what?

CODY
You know, about this. Has the boss seen any of the reels yet?

CHLOE
I don't know. Maybe.

CODY
Has he made up his mind?

CHLOE
I wouldn't know.

(CHLOE addresses others, who stop to listen as volume returns to normal.)

CHLOE
OK, listen up everybody. We're going to take a few minutes and relax. Regroup.

WARD (drinking)
Yeah, why don't we go ahead and do that. Let's take a break.

CHLOE
Right. That's what I said.

WARD
Next you'll be telling us when to eat. When to sleep.

CHLOE
If it makes for a better show . . .

WARD
But you'll never give us our money though, will you?

CHLOE
We've been through that already.

WARD
You have. You've been through it. I've been through the wringer.

SARA
(to WARD)
It's not just you, it's all of us.

CHLOE
(getting the idea)
Look, if you want to quit . . .

WARD
Who said anything about quitting?

CHLOE
You seem disgruntled is all.

WARD
Dis—?

CHLOE
If you'd rather put an end to this whole . . .

WARD
Charade? This whole charade?

CHLOE
I don't know what you're talking about.

WARD
That's it isn't it? That's how you work it.

CHLOE
Work what?

WARD
You probably had it all rigged from the start.

CHLOE
I'm afraid you got it all wrong.

CODY
Why would we rig the competition? We don't gain anything.

CHLOE
That's right. What he said.

WARD
I don't know how you . . . your inner workings. Probably obligated to come here or some such thing. You probably had a winner already picked. Probably some relative.

CHLOE
I can assure you that's not the case.

CODY
Truth is you all do have some stiff competition.

WARD
(to others)

See? You see there? I was right.

CHLOE
(exasperated)
Look, if it's down to you people, a house full of sex workers, and a clan of circus freaks, who do you think finishes third?

(Pause.)

WARD
I see.

CHLOE
I mean come on. Look at you all. You're pathetic, sure, but you're just not that interesting.

SARA
(relieved)
Thank god for that.

RITA
Ward, what is she talking about?

(Pause. WARD paces slowly, starting to seethe.)

WARD
That's how it is. We're not interesting enough.

CODY
Well, it's not that really. You're just not . . .

CHLOE
Freaks.

SARA
That's a matter of opinion.

WARD

And I thought we had some free will in the matter. But the fix was in. (beat) I see what they're up to. I see it loud and clear. (beat) Well I'm taking charge here. I'm not gonna just let things happen to me. It's my life. I decide what happens.

(Pause. WARD grabs camera off of CODY's shoulder and throws it to the ground, smashing it.)

CHLOE

Oh . . . Oh . . . Real mature!

CODY (incensed)

What the hell are you doing?

WARD

I'm ending this.

CODY

Do you have any idea how much that costs?

CHLOE

(not concerned)
It belongs to the studio. We'll write it off.

(Camera has broken open, revealing that there's no film.)

SAM

(pointing to camera)
There's nothing in there.

WARD

What do you mean?

SARA (surprised)

No film in the camera.

SAM
Oh that's hilarious.

CHLOE
(obviously faking)
Dammit, Cody, what happened to the film?

CODY
(genuinely surprised)
I put film in that camera.
    (to CHLOE)
What did you do?

CHLOE
Me? Oh please . . .

(WARD sits at kitchen table and pours a glass. RITA, stunned, tries to comfort him. SARA, angered, looks accusingly at CODY, who tries to show his innocence. She shakes her head and storms off.)

CODY (to CHLOE)
What did you do with the film?

CHLOE (resigning)
I sent it in to the boss.

RITA
You showed the film to Bruce Springsteen?

CHLOE (to CODY)
He asked for a progress report so I gave it to him. Then he told me to go through the motions, make it look legit and finish the schedule but not to waste anymore film.

(Pause. CODY kicks camera and storms out.)

                              WARD

We're not rats.

                          CHLOE (tired)

What?

                              WARD

We're not some experiment of yours. We're people you
know. I work hard . . .

                              CHLOE

There's no experiment. Look, you lost. It was decided. People
lose all the time. Today it was your turn.

                         WARD (murderous)

Don't you call us losers!

   (Pause.)

                              CHLOE

I'm just going to go.

                              RITA

Yes, maybe that's best.

   (CHLOE heads to door, pauses for a beat, then turns
back.)

                              CHLOE

Don't take it too hard. You're not any different than most
people. Maybe you just need to rethink your priorities. (beat;
brightens) And don't forget to watch us Fridays at eight!

   (CHLOE exits.)

                    RITA
Maybe she's right. Maybe for people like us, these kind of dreams are more than we can afford.

(RITA gets a glass and sits down next to WARD at the table. She pours herself a drink. SAM also pours himself a drink, then chuckles bitterly.)

                    WARD
   (to SAM)
What's so damn funny?

                    SAM
You. Looks like your boat just sunk.

                RITA (warning)
Sam . . .

                    SAM
Cutting up newspapers to get on television. There's a brilliant idea.

                    WARD
   (growing angry)
I don't need to hear anything from you.

                    SAM
   (looking at camera on ground)
And no one was even paying attention.

                    WARD
At least I made an effort. I'm trying to keep this family together.

                SAM (laughing)
You thought this really mattered. You thought you could control the situation.

                    RITA

Ward, please don't—

                    WARD

    (to RITA)
Don't tell me what to do. Everybody's been telling me what to do and I'm sick of it. I've worked my whole life and I got nothing to show for it! Nothing.

                    RITA

    (to WARD)
What do you mean, "nothing?"

                    WARD

You try to take care of your family, try to be a man—

                    SAM

Oh yeah, you were the man. You took control.

    (WARD slaps SAM hard. SAM is stunned.)

            WARD (menacingly)

You . . .
    (WARD punctuates his speech with blows, perhaps with a chair, to SAM, who gradually crouches until he's cowering on the floor.)
You're no good on the deck of a boat, no good in a marriage, and no use as a son.

    (WARD straightens. Silence. SAM is crouched in a fetal position. WARD walks to kitchen table and pours himself another drink.)

             RITA (bitterly)

Ward.
    (Pause.)

Sam?

BLACKOUT

Scene 6

(SAM stands wearing his superhero costume on his legs, though it's folded at his waist, only half on. He wears a T-shirt and holds a telephone. Farther off, MEREDITH stands holding a phone. She's dressed normally. Nothing else on stage is visible.

As the scene progresses, they will gradually circle closer to one another until they face each other.)

SAM

Before I . . . left the house, I boxed up a few of your things.

MEREDITH (surprised)

Really.

SAM

I thought it might help. You know. To deal with it.

MEREDITH

What did you pack?

SAM

But it didn't. Help. I mean, each time I closed a lid, I felt like I'd packed away a part of me. I felt like I was taking off a piece of myself and locking it away where I'd never get it back. And if I kept doing it, if I kept breaking off pieces and packing them away, I'd end up with a bunch of boxes and nothing left of who I was.

(Pause.)

But now I wonder. Maybe in the end, that's not such a bad thing, you know? Breaking off pieces of myself, of who I was. I'd just have to be willing to face whatever's left. Or not left, I guess.

(Pause. MEREDITH fights back tears.)

SAM
You still there?

(At first she just nods.)

MEREDITH
Yeah. (beat) How long do you plan on staying in a motel?

SAM
I don't know. Not long I guess. (beat) I didn't know where to go.

MEREDITH
Why don't you just go home?

SAM
Home. (beat) I don't know why he still gets to me. You'd think by now I could live with it.

MEREDITH
Your father?

SAM
And one of my greatest fears has always been that one day I'd end up like him.

MEREDITH
You're nothing like your father, Sam.

SAM
But I don't know if I'll ever know for sure. Seems like so much depends on how others see us. What they think of us.

MEREDITH
It shouldn't.

SAM
But it does. Others make us, others tear us down. And life is all in your point of view. (beat) I thought we were happy. I thought I was a good husband.

(Pause.)

MEREDITH
You're going to feel better, Sam.

SAM
I know. (beat) Tell me something.

MEREDITH
Not now, Sam, I really don't want to get into all this—

SAM
No, this is something different. Something I've been wanting to know. (beat) What do you hear when there isn't any sound?

MEREDITH
I'm not sure I understand.

SAM
When everything's quiet, and you're still. Do you hear things in the silence?

MEREDITH
Wouldn't that mean it's not silent anymore?

SAM
Well, I suppose, but that's not the point. (beat) Forget it.

MEREDITH
But is it ever really silent? Is that what you're asking?

SAM

I guess so. Maybe.

MEREDITH

Can you ever really experience complete silence?

SAM

Actually, I don't know. I think that's part of what I'm—

MEREDITH

Because if you did, I think you'd be onto something.

SAM

Onto what?

MEREDITH

If I knew that . . .
    (Pause.)
This won't last, you know that, right?

SAM

What won't?

MEREDITH

Any of it.

    (They are facing each other. Long pause. SAM raises a hand slowly, and it's mirrored by MEREDITH, as if she's a reflection.)

SAM

The basil is dying. Outside the back door.

MEREDITH

Did you water it? If it hasn't rained you need to water it.

    (Pause.)

SAM
When did we all grow so far apart from one another?

MEREDITH
I think life does that to us all on its own.

SAM
We don't need to make it so easy. (beat) Goodbye, Mer.

MEREDITH
Goodbye . . . Sam?

(MEREDITH disappears and SAM's screen goes dark. After a moment, the slithering-crawling sound comes from outside once again, followed by the thump of a heartbeat. SAM, frightened, stares at door, then rummages for his headphones and puts them on. He opens up computer again. He pushes buttons but the screen remains dark. When the noises reach their peak, he smashes the laptop over his knee.)

BLACKOUT

Scene 7

(Much later that evening, into early morning. Light on WARD sitting at kitchen table with glass and bottle of liquor. He's been there awhile. SAM, dimly seen, enters through front door.)

WARD

You're supposed to live by certain rules. They tell you to do things one way – work hard, raise a family. Then what? Still get screwed. Carpet gets pulled right out from under. (beat) Somebody somewhere's getting a real good laugh. And it sure as hell ain't me.
(Pause.)
And women make no goddamn sense. Supposed to read their minds. Supposed to do what they want without them having to actually speak. I mean, hell, what good are words if half the people don't want to use them right?
(Lights come up slightly on SAM, who's wearing a fisherman's bib and boots. He's wet, and dragging a sack behind him.)
And they all want Prince Charming to come along and sweep them off . . . Take care of things. (snorts) Horse shit. Prince Charming just needs to look good when they want him to, then shut up and carry the heavy loads. He's gotta do what he's told and keep his mouth shut. Turns out Prince Charming is a goddamn butler.
(WARD turns to SAM.)
You know what I'm saying. Your marriage went under. You should know exactly what I'm talking about. (beat) What the hell is wrong with you anyway? Soaking wet.
(looking more closely)
What are you wearing?

(SAM picks up the massive sack and empties it on the table in front of WARD. Hundreds of clams spill out over the table and onto the floor.)

SAM
They were there all right, just like you said. Got a whole dredge full of them.

   (SAM gets a glass out of a cupboard, pours a drink from the bottle and sits at the table with WARD.)

WARD
You offload the cage by yourself?
   (SAM nods; WARD is quietly impressed. Pause.)
I only ever wanted what's best for you, boy.
   (Pause. SAM stands still, watching WARD.)
Fair enough.

   (SAM relaxes and sits at table.)

WARD
There was a bar in Dutch Harbor, a little shack called the Elbow Room where the crabbers stood ankle deep in bills. They'd come from the docks with rolls bulging their pockets, and if they dropped anything under a fifty, it just wasn't worth bending over to pick up. But the bottom fell out before I could get there. Right before you were born.

SAM
Bottom fell out of the Bering when I was in college.

WARD
What are you talking about? That isn't the way it was at all. You don't even know.

SAM
I know exactly what I'm talking about. You're rewriting the past.

(RITA quietly comes out onto top of stairs, listens, and descends.)

WARD

What do you know? You don't know shit. You have it easy. Just run around doing whatever the hell you want. Pouring coffee. You don't have to do anything not to survive anyway. "Rewriting the past." How about when you have a wife and kids? Have to put food on the table? What then? What do you know about that?
(Pause.)
Think I wanted to fish? Think I wanted to stand in the freezing rain or hot sun all these years? Hell. (to self) I just never knew what else to do. (louder) That's not taking the easy way out. That's doing what you know you gotta do.

RITA

But I never asked you to, Ward. I just wanted us to be happy. I never cared what you did, or what you called yourself.

(Pause.)

WARD

We could lose the goddamn house.

SAM

You've been in tough spots before.

WARD

Yeah, one after the other. They never end. It's been a life full of tough spots.

RITA

No it isn't. I know you don't believe that.
(RITA stands next to WARD, holding his head.)
We'll make it out of this. But you're going to have to make an effort. With us. You have to try. I can't take any more

nonsense. You need to wake up. We all need to wake up around here.
(Pause. RITA looks around, takes out a piece of paper, writes something on it and sticks it on the top of WARD's head.)
Sam, are you planning on cleaning up these clams?

BLACKOUT

Scene 8

(Later. House dimly lit. Spotlight on SAM seated on cushion in living room. Perhaps we can barely hear crickets. Nothing happens for at least a minute. Then, quietly at first and building louder, we hear the same noises from before: murmuring and movement, though the heartbeat sound is normal, not rapid.

The noise builds until it again sounds as if it's at the front door. SAM, unafraid, finally stands and walks over to the door. After a pause, he opens the door.

Nothing is there. He slowly closes the door, locks the deadbolt, and returns to the cushion. He sits for a few moments and the sounds don't return. The lights slowly fade to the sound of crickets.)

Scene 9

(The next day. SAM sits at table shucking corn from a pile of ears and dumping them into a large pot. Another large pot also is on the table, and a few clams are still scattered on the floor and table. SARA sits across from SAM sipping from a mug, watching, fascinated.)

SARA
OK, I think I got it: You were trying to throw clams into the pot from across the room and missed a lot. Is that it?

SAM
Something like that.

(Pause.)

SARA
So you're not really thinking of buying Dad's boat, are you?

SAM
I'm considering it.

SARA
What for? You're not gonna fish with it.

SAM
You never know. (beat) Probably not. I'm thinking more along the lines of an extended trip. There are a lot of places I've never been.

SARA
You're just going to sail off by yourself?

SAM
Not by myself, I'm thinking of getting a dog. (beat) Look, I've thought about it and the truth is the house is too big for

just me now. Plus, I think I've lost my fondness for the smell of coffee. (beat) I'm selling all of it.

   (Pause.)

SARA
Did you find whatever you were looking for? When you left?

SAM
I think I did, at least a little. I mean, I think I heard something. Or rather, I might've heard a little bit of nothing.

SARA
Perhaps, if you tried, you could make less sense.

SAM
Well, what I heard was not totally nothing, exactly. There was something to hear out there for sure. Something quiet but . . . vast. Like listening to space. Like holding the world's largest seashell up to your ear. But that "out there" was more "in here" the whole time (pointing to head).

SARA
Yeah. Not really following.

SAM
Out on the water, in the middle of a fog and with night coming on, I couldn't see a thing. I could hear the waves lapping at the boat, maybe a buoy bell once in a while. I was pulling up the trawl, and I just stopped. Everything was still, like the world was just waiting. And all I was doing was noticing it. Nothing else. It felt like everything and nothing at the same time.
   (Pause.)
For a minute there was nothing but awareness. No "me." Nothing in between.

(SAM goes back to shucking.)

SARA

And?

SAM

Then nothing. As soon as I noticed it, everything passed and my stomach growled. But for a second there . . .

SARA

So what does it mean? This . . . fishing epiphany of yours.

SAM

No idea. But I'm going to work on that.

SARA

No idea?

SAM

I think it's the beginning of something. I think I've scratched a surface, and I want to spend the rest of my life scratching it harder.

SARA

Whatever you say. Can't say I get it but it sounds promising.

(Pause.)

SAM

So what's the deal with whatshisname? The camera guy?

SARA

Cody. We're going to dinner.

SAM

Really?

SARA
Really.

SAM
That's too bad. I'm making clams. (mimicking CHLOE) Kidding. (beat) So sis is finally stepping out.

SARA
It has been a while.

SAM
Yes, you're almost getting too big for your chastity belt. (beat) Cody. Sounds like a dog's name.

SARA
Does it.

SAM
A Lab. A chocolate Lab.

SARA
They happen to be among my favorite dogs.

(SARA gets up to pour more coffee into her cup.)

SAM
When are Mom and Dad supposed to be back?

SARA
She said two weeks. But don't jinx it. They're not gone yet. Dad might end up having a fit and smashing his suitcase. But maybe Mom finally has him under control now. (beat) Do you want some more coffee?

SAM
No, I'm OK.

BLACKOUT

END OF PLAY

www.ingramcontent.com/pod-product-compliance
Lightning Source LLC
Chambersburg PA
CBHW022136080426
42734CB00006B/390